Thanks

M000226917

The Art of The Mentor

The Superpower That Turns Good into Great

SUSAN SOFFER COHN

First published by Ultimate World Publishing 2020
Copyright © 2020 Susan Soffer Cohn

ISBN

Paperback: 978-1-922497-28-4
Ebook: 978-1-922497-29-1

Susan Soffer Cohn has asserted her rights under the Copyright, Designs and Patents Act 1988 to be identified as the author of this work. The information in this book is based on the author's experiences and opinions. The publisher specifically disclaims responsibility for any adverse consequences which may result from use of the information contained herein. Permission to use information has been sought by the author. Any breaches will be rectified in further editions of the book.

All rights reserved. No part of this publication may be reproduced, stored in or introduced into a retrieval system, or transmitted in any form, or by any means (electronic, mechanical, photocopying, recording or otherwise) without the prior written permission of the author. Any person who does any unauthorized act in relation to this publication may be liable to criminal prosecution and civil claims for damages. Enquiries should be made through the publisher.

Cover design: Ultimate World Publishing
Layout and typesetting: Ultimate World Publishing
Editor: Rebecca Low

Ultimate World Publishing
Diamond Creek,
Victoria Australia 3089
www.writeabook.com.au

What People Say

"After I retired, I decided to learn how to paint. Susan became my teacher, my mentor, my critic and my inspiration. She taught me to look at a canvas and not be frightened to put my brush filled with paint on it to make something that was special to me."

— **Phyllis Spear**

"To be with Susan is the opportunity to be inspired and to understand that freeing oneself is to allow reality to become beauty and joy. After all, it is said, 'Creativity is intelligence having fun.' Susan's art and teachings have lifted me and provided great fulfillment."

— **Sandra Horwitz**

"I have known Susan for decades...as a friend, a teacher, an artist, and a mentor. I value her advice and guidance and am eager to read her book!!"

— Barbara Shoag

"As an art mentor, I believe authenticity and trust are the most important. My role is not to solve their problems, but to help them build on their strengths, and to remind them of the tools they already have. Susan is one of those artists who is self-driven, highly disciplined, and has a self-confidence ready to take on the challenges of art. Her etchings display the precision and beauty that is expected in award-winning, high-end art. As her mentor in the medium of printmaking, it was my pleasure to watch Susan navigate her progress on her journey to success."

— Aurora Leos

Contents

Dedication

River of Memories

This book is dedicated to Victor. As I told you over and over, you will always be in my heart.

There are stars up above,
So far away we only see their light
Long, long after the star itself is gone.
And so it is with people that we loved—
Their memories keep shining ever brightly
Though their time with us is done.
But the stars that light up the darkest night,
These are the lights that guide us.
As we live our days, these are the ways we
remember.

**— Hannah Senesh,
in the book 'Mishkan T'Filah'**

Seventeenth Summer

It was a June evening in St. Louis, already hot and humid. Lightening bugs floated through the dusk of the evening. I was too old to chase them and put them in jars with air holes in the lid so they would survive as they became part of a lantern. We did that when we were little, but it was 1960 and I was 17.

The phone rang. Mom said it was for me...it was my cousin Frank calling me. Frank never called me. I only saw him on holidays. He was ten years older and not that interested in his younger cousins other than to say hello.

"Are you dating anybody?" he asked.

"Yeah, I am."

Well, I want you to meet my friend's little brother Victor. He's coming home from school in a couple of days," Frank explained.

"I guess that would be OK," I replied in a 17-year-old articulate.

I was dating Boots Leahy. I met him on our Junior class trip to Washington, DC. His cousin was in my class at Clayton High in suburban St. Louis. He went to Ladue High in the upscale suburb to the West.

It wasn't really serious, but he was sweet and liked taking me out. It also meant I had a date for times that I needed one. His family was wonderful to me and treated me like family from the minute I met them. Boots and I had very little in common, but he was nice to spend time with.

Then, Victor called. We talked for a while and he asked me out.

I was 17 and getting ready to go away for my last summer at camp two weeks later. It was no big deal to meet the guy my cousin wanted me to meet.

He took me to the stock car races. I had never heard of stock car races before. It was loud and dirty and new to me. It was fast and outrageous, but also exciting and I loved being somewhere so out of character for girls in my neighborhood. We had a good time. He called a couple of days later to ask me out again. This time, we went to see a movie near my house.

Soon, it was time for me to leave for the summer. We went out to breakfast and held hands and stared into each other's eyes. Then, a sign of things to come, he helped my mom pack my trunk while I sat on my bed talking to them.

We wrote to each other every day for the eight weeks that I was gone.

He was calling me "Dearest Darling" by the end of the summer.

In the letters, we told each other everything from our summer experiences, our feelings, and stories about our lives and our families. We fell in love through writing without the pressure or boredom of seeing someone every day when you are 17. We had no faults or bad habits in the mail. The letters were romantic, like a fantasy for a girl at her last summer at camp, knowing that she had to grow up very soon and that years of idyllic summers in Wisconsin were coming to an end.

The friends I had made, the leadership and skills I had learned, the songs sung and secrets told around a glowing campfire would soon be memories. My friends and I wanted to put the brakes on the days and nights that sped by and savor the last summer of our childhood. The strong oaks and weeping willows of our beautiful camp surrounded us as we stayed up all night on our last night there, trying to cling to every minute.

Victor was at St. Louis Union Station when my train arrived, standing next to my parents. I didn't know who to hug first.

The next week, he proposed. We were 17 and in love, but I thought we were a little young for marriage. He was leaving in a few weeks for his last year of military school and I was heading back to finish high school at Clayton. It was the first time he proposed, but not the last.

So, what happened to Boots? Well, that was the summer I had two marriage proposals. I explained to Boots that I couldn't marry him. He didn't understand. He said he didn't see why we shouldn't be together.

A year or two later when his mother died, he called and asked me to come to the wake and sit with the family. I told him I was dating Victor and he said he understood, but the family wanted me there. So, I sat with them, Mrs. Leahy laid out in the parlor, for a couple of days. They were just as welcoming as they had been during the spring when we were dating. I ran into him over the years and he always had that wonderful, welcoming disposition.

I had moved onto the next phase of my life.

Victor and I were married in 1963. I lost him in March of 2020. We were just as much in love as that first summer, maybe much more.

Foreword

Embarking

One thing becomes very clear as an art educator; we forget to play, to engage with our surroundings without a worry or care. I asked my drawing students recently, "Who drew as a child?" All hands went up. "Who draws now?" I asked. The hands were sparse.

As we grow up, we lose the beauty and power of drawing and creating, visually documenting our position in the world in any form, raw or refined. Sensing and understanding the world through sight, touch and mind to get in touch with the creative process on a visceral level, to become joyfully absorbed in the act of making, trusting the process, totally absorbed in one's own private world.

The creative process moves forward and grows, it sharpens, nurtures and fills the heart as well as taking the head to the gym for a vital workout. It teaches us to see, to feel and respond. We do not have to do much at all, just surrender and let things happen and remember to play, just be. Don't overthink it, just do it. Don't judge or have expectations, enjoy the unravelling of the visual surprise which is a direct connection to our hearts and minds. Make marks and respond to those, then make more marks. Action— reaction, move forward until it feels right. All you have to use is line, shape, tone, colour, placement and relationship of things. Making these over and over, you will eventually understand, insight will come.

Learning to be fully present, totally absorbed, connecting to the moment of interpreting and understanding a subject or object, teaches us to truly see and feel.

In today's world of electronic devices and gadgets that we use for our happiness and workplace, it is special and unique to rely solely on one's own human mechanisms for an outcome.

Mentors and teachers can inspire, encourage, demonstrate and give insights, but in reality, the best teacher is oneself. Become aware, focused and involved in the making of things and insight and knowledge of the process will be revealed. The laws of nature lie within, a gem available to everyone. pl

— Peter Lankas, Newcastle, New South Wales, Australia

Introduction
What Is Your Dream?

Seascape with Pear

"Life isn't about waiting for the storm to pass.
It's about learning to dance in the rain."
— Vivian Greene

Iam an artist with an MBA, a right brain/left brain combination. An oxymoron? I am going to share with you how this peculiar combination led to a very satisfying and successful life transition.

As I review my life ventures, I find a plethora of supportive people who helped me to find my path through each stage of my life. Sometimes, it was someone I consciously chose and other times, a mentor fell into my lap through extenuating circumstances.

Three art mentors that had the biggest impact on my life fell into both categories. Jayne Behman was a special person who changed my life after I met her through accidental circumstances.

BJ Wilson was someone who I saw, approached, and fought to become part of her circle to prove I was worthy. I worked with her for the last five years of her life and received more than I could have expected in love, support, and her belief in me.

Finally, there was Peter Lankas, the teacher who told me no over and over again, until I finally got a yes. Peter entered my life at a very difficult time when I was far from home, ill, and was losing my husband to heart disease. After he finally took me on, he became a friend, teacher, and motivator.

These stories also include the wonderful Alyson Stanfield, Aurora Leos, and David Einstein, each of whom had an impact on developing my art as a passion and a business.

As I share my stories about my experiences with these special individuals, you will be able to access the lessons I have learned as my life changed at 50 and I overcame impossible odds to become an artist. I hope that my journey will show the reader that these life lessons are not about art, but about finding and going after your dreams.

"Colleagues are a wonderful thing- but mentors, that's where the real work gets done."

— Junot Diaz

CHAPTER 1

I Can't Do This!

Bass Player

"All truth passes through three stages. First, it is ridiculed. Second, it is violently opposed. Third, it is accepted as being self-evident."
— Arthur Schopenhauer

My husband Victor was ill. He was telecommuting to work before telecommuting was a thing. When we went to our place in Palm Springs, he was more relaxed and comfortable and he wanted to move there. Moving meant I would have to sell my business, something I did not want to do.

As time passed, however, it became clear to me that he was getting worse and I had to get him away from the stresses of Los Angeles. I found a merger partner, sold my business, and we moved.

There I was, no friends, no business, no identity. My children and grandchildren were in Los Angeles. I had worked with my son and daughter-in-law daily and now I didn't see them. I was lonely and unhappy. Victor immediately got involved in volunteering in the community. He seemed busy and happy. I found a therapist.

One Friday afternoon, Victor walked into the house and called out, "Are you dressed? There's someone here I want you to meet."

It was Sidney.

In his prime, Sidney was a Hollywood writer. He was retired and lived in a mobile home in the desert. He used to teach a creative writing class at the Senior Center, but now he was even retired from that.

Victor set up a couple of chairs by the pool, brought us something to drink, and disappeared into the house. Sidney and I talked about books, writers, and writing for a couple of hours. It was the best conversation I had had since the move. After asking me about my writing history, he suggested I try to write a children's book. After more discussion, he said he was at the Senior Center on Tuesdays and when I had a draft completed, to bring it to show him. The following Tuesday, I was there with my completed draft.

After several weeks of work, both with Sidney and a writing group he had found for me, I felt I was getting close to having something marketable. In order to think about marketing, I believed that I needed some rough sketches of the characters I had developed, but I couldn't draw. I thought I needed to find an illustrator to help me out.

At about the same time, we were invited to a fundraising auction. Victor had spotted an item on the silent auction that included four art lessons. He bid on it and presented it to me at the end of the evening.

A couple of days later, I called about the lessons. I said I had no experience and no talent. A class was starting that week, so with little hope of success, I agreed to go. I was given a list of supplies to bring and showed up at the appointed time.

Change Your Thinking
Change Your Life

- What or who holds you back from doing what you really want?

_____
_____
_____
_____
_____
_____
_____
_____
_____
_____
_____
_____
_____
_____

- At what age did you stop trying new things?

_____

_____

_____

_____

_____

_____

_____

_____

_____

_____

_____

_____

_____

_____

_____

"The artist has a special task: that of reminding men of their humanity and the promise of their creativity."
— Lewis Mumford

CHAPTER 2

The Magic of Jayne

Horses Running Wild

"One of the greatest values of mentors is the ability to see ahead what others cannot see and to help them navigate a course to their destination."
— John C. Maxwell

Jayne Behman, the owner of the gallery and art school, asked me what my goal was for the four lessons. I told her I hoped to be able to draw some rounded stick figures to show someone how to illustrate my book. I then got my first drawing lesson. The assignment was to draw a tube. I had no idea what to do, but she said it was all simple tricks, I just had to learn them. After the four lessons, during which I felt like I was all thumbs, I asked Jayne if she thought I could learn to draw very simple figures and she said yes.

For the next series of lessons, I bought acrylics and canvas and began to learn to paint. I started to create characters as I learned. After I was satisfied with one character, Jayne said, "You're doing really well, but in order to continue and grow and learn the skills to help you do a good job on your book, you need to do a serious painting."

I bought oils and started a "serious" painting. It took me two months to complete it, and each week there was another lesson about color theory, creating depth, brush strokes, and on and on.

After finishing the painting, I went back to the acrylics and my illustrations. I learned about the effects that create a sense of fun and childishness. After another month or two, Jayne said it was time for me to learn more lessons from a serious painting...back to the oils.

This process continued and before I knew it, a year had gone by. I was painting every week with a terrific group of people who were learning and growing artistically. In between classes, I worked at home for hours each day. I no longer felt out of place or lonely.

One day, at the end of the year, I walked into the studio laughing. "What are you laughing about?" Jayne asked me.

"Someone outside just asked me if I was an artist," I replied.

"What did you say?" she inquired.

"I said no of course," I told her.

"I never want to hear you say that again," Jayne told me. "Susan, have you looked at your work lately?"

That's how I found out I was an artist. It was all an accident compounded by the tricks of a master teacher along with the needs of a lonely woman trying to find a new life.

I haven't seen Sidney in many years and Jayne has become not only a mentor but a close friend. I have traveled to the Central Coast of California and to Italy to paint with Jayne and other friends I met through her and I still paint every day.

As my first art mentor, she encouraged, cajoled, suggested, and exposed me to others I could learn from.

The year following my discovery that Jayne had turned me into an artist and surprised me with the results, she began to push me out into the art world of the Coachella Valley where Palm Springs is located for an art competition. My second-place win at the National Date Festival was a beginning.

Then, there was a Friday evening art walk to the galleries along Palm Canyon Drive. Jayne offered me a studio in her gallery to show my work and I started making some first Friday sales. As other opportunities to show came up, Jayne not only told me about them but encouraged me to take them, and often we both participated in the shows as they came along.

She would bring in experts for workshops in fields like Encaustics and Perspective. I couldn't get enough.

Change Your Thinking
Change Your Life

- Has someone in your life suggested you could be more than you think?

_____

_____

_____

_____

_____

_____

_____

_____

_____

_____

_____

_____

_____

_____

_____

- Has anyone taken the time to tell you something about you that is special?

_____

_____

_____

_____

_____

_____

_____

_____

_____

_____

_____

_____

_____

_____

_____

- What was your reaction if it happened?

_____

_____

_____

_____

_____

_____

_____

_____

_____

_____

_____

_____

_____

_____

_____

_____

_____

"Always dream and shoot higher than you know how to. Don't bother just to be better than your contemporaries or predecessors. Try to be better than yourself."
— William Faulkner

CHAPTER 3

Settling into New Life

Ballroom

"Show me a successful individual and I'll show you someone who had real positive influences in his or her life. I don't care what you do for a living—if you do it well I'm sure there was someone cheering you on or showing the way. A mentor."

— Denzel Washington

Joining a New Community

From the first day we moved to Palm Springs, we realized our idyllic little condo, perfect for weekends, was full and there was no room for a lifetime of stuff. We didn't need everything that we had accumulated along the journey, but many treasures represented precious memories. I was not ready to let go.

Thus, we started to look for a house. My first priority was a view. As I was living in one of the most beautiful places on earth with desert surrounded by craggy mountains and multicolored hills, I wanted to be able to feast on the vision of it from inside and outside of a residence. Victor wanted space for his tools and hobbies.

We looked and looked, driving through one neighborhood after another and haunting open houses. At last, I saw a for sale sign on a beautiful house in an older neighborhood near our condo. I was certain that the price would be out of reach.

We went to an open house there a few days later and when we walked in, we fell in love. The house was perfect for us and the realtor was a dream. She became a good friend. We were pleasantly surprised at the asking price for the house and made an offer immediately. During the negotiations, the realtor invited me to join a women's group that she belonged to and thought I would like.

It turned out that most of my good friends in Palm Springs I met through that group. At my first meeting, I found people friendly and welcoming. After one conversation, in particular, a woman said to me, "I think you're interesting. Let's have lunch."

That lunch led to a friendship that opened more doors to me and has lasted lovingly until today. Miriam Bent and her husband Nat lived a couple of blocks from our new house. We got together a couple of times and saw each other at meetings. Then, one day she called and sounded dreadful. "I have just been diagnosed with diabetes," Miriam said. "I have never exercised in my life and the doctor says I have to start. Would you walk with me in the morning?"

I had been looking for a walking buddy. Those morning walks continued for years with lots of talking, gossiping, and collaborating on upcoming projects. It also built strength and endurance in both of us. In the hot summer, we walked back and forth in the swimming pool to keep up the exercise.

Miriam was the editor of the Jewish Newspaper in the Coachella Valley. After a few weeks, she asked me if I would write a column for the paper. What a gift that turned out to be!

I began writing a genealogy column, telling stories about my large family and my family history. After each story, I would write a brief lesson about how others could trace their family history. My photo was in the paper each month, so people started recognizing me when I was out, and started conversations with questions and comments about the column. I got calls from people who knew members of my family from the past, and from others with questions, such as, "How can I trace my family if I'm adopted?"

I always tried to find an answer and get back to them if I didn't know at the moment.

I also heard from members of my large family from all over the country. Many people living in Palm Springs and surrounding communities live somewhere else during the hot summer months. When I mentioned a cousin who lived in Florida or Illinois or Minnesota, or South Dakota, someone who read my column knew him/her from back home and called or sent the column.

In one case, two of my cousins traveled to Lithuania on a roots research trip, looking for records of great-grandparents. They went to the clerk of a small community to ask if they had any information about our family. The clerk went into his file and pulled out one of my columns about a first cousin of my grandmother's who had come from Lithuania. What are the chances of something like that happening? I guess when we put ourselves out in the world, that world can get smaller and more intimate.

During our morning walks, Miriam and I planned a summer discussion series that she had led for several years. We worked on themes, locations, speakers, and topics. She was also my advisor on what to wear for which social occasion. We could have attended events every night of the week if we chose to do so. Palm Springs is a very social place. There was definitely an unspoken dress code that I could not fathom at first.

We shopped together and pulled outfits together for every occasion. I had not had the fun of having a buddy to share discussions about clothes with since my Aunt Ruth picked all my clothes years before.

Since moving away from Palm Springs, Miriam and I still try to talk regularly. When I had my first solo art show in

Huntington Beach, Miriam and Nat were there. We miss seeing each other daily, but still value a friendship that started years ago.

Change Your Thinking
Change Your Life

- Have you ever moved to a new community where you knew nobody?

_____

_____

_____

_____

_____

_____

_____

_____

_____

_____

_____

_____

_____

_____

_____

- How did you begin to find friends and colleagues?

_____

_____

_____

_____

_____

_____

_____

_____

_____

_____

_____

_____

_____

_____

_____

_____

_____

"I need to feel the excitement of life stirring around me, and I will always need to feel that."

— William Faulkner

CHAPTER 4

One Electrifying Day
with David

Windswept

"The greatest good you can do for another is not just to share your riches but to reveal to him his own."

— Benjamin Disraeli

*A*rt class was like a day of both relaxed meditation and fun for me. One day during class, Jayne, the owner of the studio, was going back and forth between the group and an artist I hadn't met whose work she was planning to feature in her gallery. They were discussing the future show.

In the middle of the class, she came in and said, "David has agreed to talk with you for a while about abstract art." David was David Einstein, a New York abstract painter who moved to the desert to work because it was affordable both for living and working. He had a home and a large studio in Palm Springs.

There were five of us in the class. The others listened politely as he lectured about abstract art. I was completely involved and enchanted with the concepts. When he finished the lecture, I grilled him with questions.

How do you get the confidence to escape from the objective? How do you plan an abstract painting? And on and on. After that class, I knew I had to learn more about what he knew. A few months later, Jayne said she didn't have anything else to teach me at the time, but told me I should call David to see if he would teach me.

David was pretty busy. He worked day and night, taught at the local college where his classes were impacted, and took his work back to New York to show it. But when I called him, he asked me what I was doing the following Saturday. I told him whatever it was could be changed.

That's how one of the most amazing days of my life was planned.

I arrived at David's studio at the assigned time with paintings in tow. I brought them in and he asked who had painted them. I told him I had.

"Wow, they're pretty good," he said. Then, he pointed out some things I had to learn to take them to the next step. "Separate your colors more," he said. "They're getting a little muddy in here." He made a couple of other suggestions then told me I was dressed too well to paint. He said there were some old clothes in the bathroom and told me to go change.

When I came out, he was stapling a huge canvas to the wall. It had a large painting started on it. "Let me show you how I mix my paints," he said and started to demonstrate, putting the paints in a large bucket and handing me a stick for stirring.

"Have you ever painted unstretched?" David asked. I said I hadn't, so he explained why and how he did it. He painted on canvas from a roll not yet attached to stretcher bars.

When the paint was mixed, he pulled out a large brush and said, "Paint."

"It's your painting, what do you want me to do?" I asked.

"You'll know," he answered and sat down in a chair behind me, smiling silently as I painted. After a while, I said, "OK, I think I'm done with this color."

He mixed another bucket of paint, handed me an even larger brush, and stapled another large canvas on the wall. Then, the same drill. I painted until I thought I was done.

When I finished, David said, "Get dressed, we're going to the museum."

"I'm covered with paint." I protested.

"Be proud of it. You're an artist," he said.

I changed into my own clothes and off we went to the Desert Museum where they were showing an exhibit of mid-century modern painters from the Whitney Museum in New York.

We spent the afternoon walking through the museum. David told me personal stories about each of the artists and what I had to learn from the work of each. After viewing all the work on exhibit from the Whitney, he started these very personal lessons about the paintings in the museum's permanent collection.

Finally, he said, "Let's get a cup of coffee."

We sat down and went over the lessons again and then just talked about art and painting. "Do it every day if you're serious about being an artist."

"I do," I replied.

Every time I saw David from that day on, he asked, "Are you painting every day?"

I would say yes and he would hug me and tell me to keep it up.

That fantastic day influenced my work from then on, even after Victor and I moved away from the desert. I will never forget the lessons I learned and the outstanding skill of the teacher and artist I feel so privileged to know.

Postscript

Every year, Jayne held a fundraiser to bring in money to support her program to bring art to children in the Coachella Valley. Once I got good enough, she invited me to contribute my work to the silent auction. We always attended and bought something as we liked to support the program. I served on the board of her organization for years.

Some years ago, David Einstein donated a painting to the auction. His paintings sell for a lot, but I was hoping to be able to buy it. I went to Jayne in the middle of the evening and said, "I want David's painting."

"You can't have it, I already promised it to someone else," she said.

"Who is it? Maybe I can arrange to buy it after the auction."

"It isn't anybody you know. He's not here." She replied.

I was really unhappy. I complained to Victor. I complained to Jayne. I probably even complained to David.

After the evening, I called to try to get it, or at least find out who bought it. Jayne, who had become a good friend by then, wouldn't even discuss it with me. When I went there to take a class, the painting was at the studio. She still wouldn't tell me who bought it. Finally, Victor came to pick me up and they put the painting in the car. Victor had bought the painting to surprise me for our anniversary.

It hangs in our living room and is a prized treasure.

Change Your Thinking
Change Your Life

- What different scenarios could a line like, "Let's get a cup of coffee" turn into?

_____

_____

_____

_____

_____

_____

_____

_____

_____

_____

_____

_____

_____

- Have you spent time with someone who encouraged you to be proud of your work? If so, how did it make you feel?

_____

_____

_____

_____

_____

_____

_____

_____

_____

_____

_____

_____

_____

_____

_____

- Has a casual encounter ever turned into a meaningful experience? When it was happening, did you realize it was an important moment?

_____

_____

_____

_____

_____

_____

_____

_____

_____

_____

_____

_____

_____

_____

_____

"Short as I am, I played the tallest queen in history. I thought tall, I felt tall—and I looked tall."

— Helen Hayes

CHAPTER 5

Explosive Growth with Alyson

End of the Day

"If you hear a voice within you say, 'you can't paint' then by all means paint and that voice will be silenced."
— Vincent Van Gogh

It may seem the height of conceit to assume my work was worthy of all this effort, hard work, and the search for mentors, but two factors convinced me to proceed. One: I have learned that success has more to do with showing up than natural talent and ability. Two: art is, as it turns out, 90% hard work and 10% talent.

I was showing and selling my work in Palm Springs, then we moved to Huntington Beach to be closer to our children and grandchildren. I started to search out the local art community. The Huntington Beach Art League is a large, vibrant community of talented artists. They welcomed me and offered opportunities for competition, showing work, and working with wonderful people.

In addition to being accepted into juried shows, I began to win awards for my work. I was able to schedule a solo show at the Corner Gallery in the beautiful Huntington Beach Central Library.

I was pleased and surprised that I sold eight pieces at the opening reception. My new friends assured me that this result was unusual for this venue. As things progressed, I realized I was being taken seriously and it was probably time to show my work some respect and find ways to expose it to other audiences.

While looking for advice from those with more experience in the art world, I met Alyson Stanfield online. Alyson was offering a free series of art business lessons. I ordered the lessons and the teaching manual, printed them out and gathered a small group of artists who agreed to meet weekly to study the lessons together.

We took each lesson seriously and did the assignments as they were given. By the time we finished the nine weeks, the group offered to help me with a marketing plan for a show I had signed up to do in Las Vegas that would last several days. We practiced how we would set up the booth, what would be said by whom when people entered the booth, and how we would follow-up after the initial contact.

For my first art fair experience, I was delighted that the plan worked. Many artists in booths around mine did not sell anything while I had sales each day.

I had not imagined that I would be starting a career at this stage in my life, but my children were grown, my husband was supportive, and this new venture became as much a passion as anything I have ever done or attempted before. It has continued to be an important part of every day.

Alyson's advice and our planning had opened the door to selling work outside of the immediate area.

My next encounter with Alyson was a multi-day workshop held in Portland, Oregon some years later. When I spoke with her to see if the event was a good fit for me, she said the people who were attending were all serious artists with established businesses. For not the first or last time, I fought my way into the group. I believe that when you surround yourself with winners, you are more likely to become one.

It was a truly inspiring bunch. I am still in touch with many of them today. Trudy Rice is selling textiles with her artwork on them throughout Australia and beyond. Miriam Schulman has an international online art school business. Just sharing those days and hearing their stories, plus the lessons provided by Alyson, gave me the incentive and energy to reach higher.

Change Your Thinking
Change Your Life

- Do you believe your education is complete?

_____

_____

_____

_____

_____

_____

_____

_____

_____

_____

_____

_____

_____

_____

- Do you regularly search out books and/or classes so you can expand your knowledge base?

_____

_____

_____

_____

_____

_____

_____

_____

_____

_____

_____

_____

_____

_____

_____

- What other ways do you seek out enrichment of ideas? Do you travel? Do you attend seminars?

_____

_____

_____

_____

_____

_____

_____

_____

_____

_____

_____

_____

_____

_____

_____

_____

- Have you ever had to fight your way into a program you thought you needed? What happened?

_____

_____

_____

_____

_____

_____

_____

_____

_____

_____

_____

_____

_____

_____

_____

"Art is idea. It is not enough to draw, paint, and sculpt. An artist should be able to think."

— Gurdon Woods

CHAPTER 6

Mind-blowing Meeting Mastery

Collograph #10 Garden

"Mentoring is a brain to pick, an ear to listen, and a push in the right direction."
— John Crosby

et me tell you about an exceptional meeting I attended one evening at the Huntington Beach Art League. It is a large and successful art group that meets monthly. Each month, members submit artwork for competition and the speaker chooses the award winners for the month. This group often had between one hundred and two hundred pieces in competition each month.

On the night in question, the speaker was scheduled to be BJ Wilson, an accomplished artist who had exhibited and taught worldwide. I had never met BJ and did not know her work.

When the meeting began, I was delighted to see a blue ribbon on the painting I had brought to the meeting, but it got even better. During her demonstration, she not only did a fantastic painting but articulately taught as she painted and taught a technique I had never seen before. In addition, she explained why each piece that she gave a ribbon deserved to win. I learned more during that meeting than all the rest of the meetings I had attended over the past year put together. The technique was explained so well that I could go back to my studio and immediately use what she taught to improve my work.

I must admit that since I started art so late, I was very picky about choosing art teachers, and after watching her,

I was determined to study with this incredible artist. I got her card and tried to gather the courage to call her and do whatever it took to study with her.

When I did call, she said that she only took on very few students and that she was on her way to Spain with a group to paint for several weeks. "Call me when I return and we will discuss it again," she said.

So, then I had to get brave enough to call her again. When I did so, she told me that I could come to her small group once and we would see how we got along and if we were a good fit. They met in a gallery about a half-hour from my house and with much trepidation, I gathered my painting materials assembled from her required list and drove to the first meeting.

I nervously set up my easel and got out my paints. What a day! I felt a little awkward at first, but what happened next was pretty miraculous. We clicked immediately and I felt that her lessons were the logical next step for me. She said, "You are good, but you are inconsistent. I will teach you things that will make all your paintings good." She proceeded to show me things that were consistent in the work of great painters. In fact, after studying with her for a period of time, I found that I saw paintings differently when I went to a gallery or museum. Often, if I listened to a recording as I toured an exhibit, I found that I was seeing things that were not mentioned on the recordings. BJ's tips described what I saw much better than the museum pros had presented them.

When I got ready to hang a show, BJ would come to my house, help me to measure the allotted space for the show on the floor of my living room and help me to create a show on the floor, configured the same way it would be hung in the gallery.

She also was very particular about framing and matting and taught me innumerable lessons on how to make the work shine. The matting must be white (for works on paper) to go into a show. BJ made it clear that there are different colors of white and showed me the difference it made to have the correct color of white to enhance each painting.

BJ challenged me constantly and consistently for the next five years. She believed in me as no one else had. When I was being treated for breast cancer, my husband would drop me off with a few supplies and no energy, and somehow when he came back to get me, she always got me to accomplish something I had never done before.

We became great friends and colleagues. I felt so fortunate to have her in my life. She believed in me so much that I worked even harder on my work. When she gave a lesson on focus, she started using me as her example. Apparently, focus is my superpower. Then, she started photographing some of my work to include in her teaching slide set, which was mainly made up of works of the greats.

As new people joined the group, she started asking me to work with them. She taught me to teach. BJ died five years after I met her. She had profoundly altered my life.

Why go to professional association meetings?

Why would I encourage you to go to meetings that could be less than interesting? Here's the secret. It's all about the one-on-one conversations before others arrive and the networking during the coffee break.

One of the best places to find a mentor is a professional association. I didn't know I was meeting a mentor the night I met BJ Wilson. Most art meetings have demonstrations, some with lessons. Many excellent artists are unfortunately poor speakers. Often the meetings are dull unless there is an excellent programming vice-president. But usually, the program and the speakers are not the most important part of the meeting.

These are some tips to get the most out of any professional association experience.

1. Arrive early
2. Take business cards
3. Bone up on your networking skills.
4. Act like a host

When you arrive early, you are taking the opportunity to meet people when it is quiet. Volunteering to help is a great way to get into conversations with active members as well. They often know where the opportunities are. This networking time is the best part of any meeting, so get there early and greet everyone who comes in.

When you exchange business cards with someone, immediately write a note on the back of the card to remind you what you discussed and any follow up required. For the electronic savvy, take notes on your phone right away. A photo of a business card is safe on your phone and won't get lost in a pile of papers.

Becoming a good networker involves acting as a host. Greet people warmly, as if you belong, whether you do or not. Have brief, meaningful conversations, make a note, and move on to the next person. The more people you speak with, the better chance you have of finding an opportunity to go somewhere, hear about upcoming events, and find out whether you have something of value to the member, or that person has a valuable option for you.

The second most important part of a professional association meeting is the coffee break. Once again, it gives you the chance to meet and converse with more people. If you are very fortunate, the program may even be of value.

You might want to know examples of other opportunities that came up while I was networking at the Huntington Beach Art League.

1. I was invited to join a private group that painted outside once a week.
2. I was invited to join a group that was traveling to Greece to paint.
3. I heard about a new gallery that was opening that was looking for work like mine.
4. I made some lifelong friends.

With regards to my relationship with BJ, she became my teacher and mentor for the next five years, the last five years of her life. Just before she died, she invited a few of us to her home for lunch. She had a stack of paper bags and after lunch, she asked each of us to choose some books from her extensive art library. When I got home, she called to ask which books I had chosen and seemed really happy with my choices and that they would now be in my art library.

I will never forget her kindness, her lessons, and her friendship. Among the most valuable gifts she gave me was that she slowly, patiently taught me to teach and mentor others.

Change Your Thinking
Change Your Life

- Is there a professional organization for the field you are passionate about? Do some research and write down the names and contact people in each group.

_____

_____

_____

_____

_____

_____

_____

_____

_____

_____

_____

_____

- When you go to a meeting, do you talk to the one person you know, or move around the room introducing yourself?

_____

_____

_____

_____

_____

_____

_____

_____

_____

_____

_____

_____

_____

_____

_____

Next time you go to a meeting, challenge yourself to meet 10 new people or set a higher goal for yourself. Volunteer to be a greeter or give out name tags, you will meet many people that way.

"This is the last of the human freedoms—to choose one's attitude in any given set of circumstances, to choose one's own way."
— **Viktor Frankl**

CHAPTER 7

Belief Leads to Bonus Breakthrough

From the Pier

"Our chief want in life is somebody who will make us do what we can."
— Ralph Waldo Emerson

*A*fter working with BJ for a couple of years, she told me one day that of all her students (in college, university, and private classes over many, many years), I was the one who was going to make it.

What a responsibility! It was overwhelming! How was this possible? As you now know, I was a grandmother before I took my first art lesson. I had no natural ability or experience before that, and my hands shake.

Having a brilliant artist and teacher say something like that to me took my breath away. What was she seeing that I didn't understand?

One thing became very clear, however. If she said it, I had a responsibility to make it happen. I didn't want to disappoint my mentor and now friend in any way, so I was determined to work even harder.

I set two goals...

The first was that I wanted to be on the ladder. So, what does that mean? For me, it means that we stand on the shoulders of those who have come before us, and my hope was to take my place on that ladder so that future artists can stand on mine.

One day in 2017, when I was standing in my gallery, a young woman came in and stood before a large painting of mine for a very long time. She looked and looked without saying a word. Finally, she turned to me and said do you mind if I take a photo of this painting. Most artists know that this is poor etiquette. Admiring the work of other artists is great, copying it is not copacetic.

But she went on to explain. She was a student in an excellent art program in Los Angeles. She had an assignment to build a project based on the work of an artist that inspired her and took her somewhere she had not been before. "I would like to use you as my inspiration," she said. "I will give you credit so that my professor and the other students will know where the inspiration came from." That was the day! Was I really on the ladder? It felt as if I had set a goal and reached it on that day.

BJ told me that an artist needed an auction value. So, I set that as my second goal. What does that mean? When your work is in a collection that goes to auction, there must be information online about your work such as where it has been and in what collection, and therefore what value it could bring in an auction setting. The difficulty here is that you must be auctioned to have a record of value, and many auction companies told me not to put pieces in an auction until the value is high enough to be respectable. Thus, it becomes a Catch-22, you can't have an auction value until and unless you already have an auction value.

This is a challenge I am still pursuing.

While looking through my art library the other day, I found a postcard from BJ epitomizing the mentor relationship. I will try to share the essence of it with you here.

Introduction to Art and Painting by BJ Wilson

All art forms stem from previous forms. Each new style is based on the principles underlying past art, but each new way of painting expresses the need and temper of the era in which the artist is working. The new style takes time to become accepted and when it does, the old style is looked upon as an "old hat." That is why Titian did not paint the way Giotto painted, although Giotto was a great and famous painter. Giotto's style was considered provincial in Titian's day. The society Titian lived in was different, so he invented a new

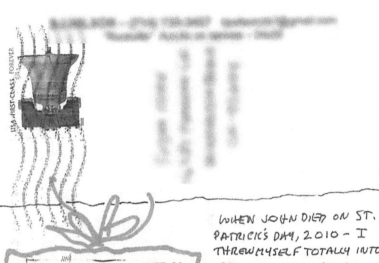

DEADLINE DECEMBER 31
Call for Collage-Based Art. 2012 marks the centennial of the appearance of collage in painting. Collage has become ubiquitous within contemporary art and culture; its myriad applications have arguably expanded its original definition to become the most inclusive artistic process. Strange Glue — Collage at 100 is a three-part exhibition series that runs from September 2012 through June 2013. All media considered. Please follow the "call for art" link at:

WHEN JOHN DIED ON ST. PATRICK'S DAY, 2010 — I THREW MYSELF TOTALLY INTO SPRUCING UP MY HOUSE — KNOWING I'D NEVER DO IT TWICE! IT TURNED OUT TO BE A FAR BIGGER THAN I'D PLANNED, & IT ISN'T DONE YET! PART OF THE SUB-FLOOR HAD TO BE REPLACED; NEW KITCHEN/BATH FLOOR, NEW CARPETS, ANOTHER SKYLIGHT, THE WHOLE L.R. THAT WENT ACROSS THE FRONT NOW TURNED INTO A STUDIO BUT NO TIME TO PAINT ANYTHING SO FAR. I LIVE IN HOPE. PLUS WANT TO DO 2 BOOKS. YOU MAY REMEMBER WE HAD A LOT OF RAIN — WHICH MEANT I NEEDED A NEW ROOF. I HADN'T PLANN ON THAT BUT WAS GLAD I COULD DO IT. PAINT INSIDE — SOME PAINT OUTSIDE; THE LIST GOES ON. SEND YOUR IMPRESSIVE RESUMÉ IF YOU CAN SEND TO THIS IN THE EAST & LET ME KNOW HOW IT TURNS OUT XX BJ

85

way of painting to express the temper of his times. Rembrandt did not paint the way Titian or Raphael did because the mood and society of his day were different, so he invented a new way of painting to express this. Each time there is a social revolution of any type, art has changed to express the new belief of man.

Although the artists work out a new way to express the change in society, they do not discard any, or all, of the painting knowledge each generation has so laboriously acquired. They simply emphasize certain qualities and change others to say what they want to say, adding any new knowledge this change has forced them to invent.

The use of certain shapes to express mood has always been a part of art knowledge over the centuries. Color has never been dependent on reality but always used symbolically for mood.

The basic problems dealing with composition have consistently confronted the artist. The control of the picture surface and the illusion of depth have always been problems. The illusion of depth was conquered by the invention of linear perspective and overlapping planes.

A line (or edge of a mass), by jumping space and becoming the edge of another mass, creates continuity and helps make each part of the picture a part of the whole. Many times, this continuity cannot easily be seen, but it is always felt. — BJ Wilson

This is a shortened summary of a much longer introduction, but it gives a sense of the history of art and how each generation stands on the shoulders of the generation before, then adds to the literature.

This speaks to me, as one of my primary goals is to be on that ladder, learning from the generations before and contributing to the future.

Change Your Thinking
Change Your Life

- Do you have a primary goal for your life? If so, write it here.

_____

_____

_____

_____

_____

_____

_____

_____

_____

_____

_____

_____

_____

_____

_____

- If not, brainstorm a few possibilities and write them down.

_____

_____

_____

_____

_____

_____

_____

_____

_____

_____

_____

_____

_____

_____

_____

_____

_____

"Every authentic work of art is a gift to the future."

— Albert Camus

CHAPTER 8

Red Light—
A Failing Formula

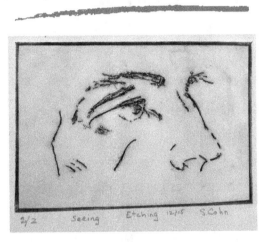

Windswept

"In order to be a mentor, and an effective one, one must care. You must care. You don't have to know how many square miles are in Idaho, you don't need to know what is the chemical makeup of chemistry, or of blood or water. Know what you know and care about the person, care about what you know and care about the person you're sharing with."
— Maya Angelou

Some years ago, I saw that a local junior college was listing a course in mixed media. It was an area of interest for me as I had been doing a lot of work in the genre and wanted to extend my knowledge. I signed up and was told I needed the permission of the instructor. I promptly made an appointment to meet him, choosing some of my work to take along.

The instructor was brusque and somewhat rude. He had no interest in seeing my work, and my guess is, he was trying to fill another of his classes. Instead of addressing my interests, he told me I had to take a course in sculpture as a prerequisite for the mixed media class. That seemed like an ok option. I had not taken a sculpture class before, so I signed up, bought the materials, and showed up for the first class.

He would come into the classroom at the minute the class started first thing in the morning and give a brief, maybe 15-minute lecture on technique, then promptly disappeared until after lunch. Many of the students were very young and even older ones were beginners. Fortunately, the more experienced students were kind enough to help the new ones. We worked all morning, took a brief lunch break, and at the exact minute we were to begin for the afternoon session, the professor reappeared. He once again spoke for about five minutes, then walked around the class and gave often brutal critiques. I saw him several times walk up to a young, budding artist, lift his hand in the air and smash the work the student had been toiling over for hours.

One after another, these young hopeful artists started disappearing from the class.

The class requirements included completing three projects during the semester in order to pass. I had a graduate degree and felt no pressure to get junior college credit, so I was under much less pressure than the 18 and 19-year-old students, but I was offended by his attitude and his absence for over 90 percent of the class time. Finally, one day after completing my three projects, I picked up my tools and started out the door. He asked where I was going, and I told him I was done. He asked what he should do with the piece I was working on. I told him to throw it away.

I told him I was too old to put up with teachers who behave in this way. It is very possible that I am just old enough that I refuse to be treated the way he treated people and more than that, I was disgusted that he was demotivating talented young people from continuing their studies.

I choose my teachers and mentors very carefully and this guy didn't make the cut.

Change Your Thinking
Change Your Life

What are the signs that you are approaching the wrong person to become your mentor? Since mentors are in a power position in the relationship, it's easy for them to commit some of the following offenses if their intentions and motivations come from the wrong place.

Signs of a bad choice! If your chosen person behaves this way, get out fast.

_____

_____

_____

_____

_____

_____

_____

_____

_____

- Does he/she take credit for your work and insert him/herself in a position of leadership on your projects?

_____

_____

_____

_____

_____

_____

_____

_____

_____

_____

_____

_____

_____

_____

_____

_____

- Does he/she insist you not develop your own work, but use you to advance his/her projects?

_____

_____

_____

_____

_____

_____

_____

_____

_____

_____

_____

_____

_____

_____

- Has this person slowed your progress by being unavailable?

_____

_____

_____

_____

_____

_____

_____

_____

_____

_____

_____

_____

_____

_____

- Have you been discouraged from seeking advice from others?

_____

_____

_____

_____

_____

_____

_____

_____

_____

_____

_____

_____

_____

_____

_____

_____

_____

- Have you been discouraged from pursuing a passion?

_____

_____

_____

_____

_____

_____

_____

_____

_____

_____

_____

_____

_____

_____

_____

_____

Run, do not walk, away from people who behave in this way.

"Keep away from people who try to belittle your ambitions. Small people always do that, but the great make you feel that you too, can become great."

— Mark Twain

CHAPTER 9

Daring to Teach

The Living Room

"I've learned a lot from mentors who were instrumental in shaping me, and I want to share what I've learned."

— Herbie Hancock

*B*J taught me to teach, but I still didn't feel qualified to teach and mentor others.

People who saw my work began asking me if I taught. One person said upon seeing an exhibit, "I have to study with you." After I had experienced this phenomenon six or seven times within a couple of months, I decided to give it a try. I called the individuals who had asked for a class and inquired if they were still interested. Within a couple of weeks, I had an enthusiastic group of five beginners ready to start. I sent out a supply list and we began.

I carefully wrote out sequential lesson plans. Our weekly meetings were fun and each person progressed at their own rate, but each was making progress. I discovered that they had different goals, expectations, and natural abilities, but they all seemed to be having a good time.

After a year of lessons, I arranged a teacher/student show at a local gallery. Each of the students invited friends. It reminded me of my first show when I was so embarrassed for anyone to see what I was showing, but was surprised at the positive comments. All of them got positive feedback and we had one sale at the opening reception. Everyone was excited about that.

Then, they all came back for another year. The class continued for three years, after which I moved out of the area. Each year, we had a show and each year, sales increased until all had sold a work they had done.

The fine training that I had received translated into an understanding that each student was different and needed encouragement and assistance from me in unique ways. What worked for one did not work for another. Keeping the class small and personal helped me to feel my way toward mentoring each one. It was so exciting for me to see how working individually with them produced results. The work of one looked nothing like the work of another. I tried to help them discover what they wanted from the classes and assist them in finding that special thing.

Some teachers do a demonstration for the class and then say do this. To me, that was counterproductive. I didn't want them to turn into copies of me. My goal was to help them become the best them.

When I moved out of the area, I encouraged them to find another teacher. Some of them are still working with that new mentor.

Change Your Thinking
Change Your Life

Studies show that a good connection between two individuals is required in a mentoring relationship. A research study designed and conducted by mentoring expert, Belle Rose Ragins, at the University of Wisconsin-Milwaukee showed that without a personal connection, there is virtually no difference between someone who is mentored and someone who is not. The best mentors go beyond imparting competency and focus on values and self-awareness. Belle Rose Ragins is a professor of management at the University of Wisconsin-Milwaukee. Her research interests focus on mentoring, diversity and positive relationships at work.Her work appears in professional journals and she has co-authored a number of books on these subjects.

- Have you chosen a mentor who goes beyond imparting competency?

_____

_____

_____

_____

_____

_____

_____

_____

_____

_____

_____

_____

_____

_____

_____

_____

_____

_____

- Does your chosen mentor focus on values and self-awareness? In what way?

_____

_____

_____

_____

_____

_____

_____

_____

_____

_____

_____

_____

_____

_____

_____

_____

"The artist need not know very much, best of all let him work instinctively and paint as naturally as he breathes or walks."

— Emil Nolde

CHAPTER 10
Trade-Off Produces Remarkable Results

She was Smart Before She Married

"If I have seen further it is by standing on the shoulders of giants."

— Isaac Newton

For a few years, we set out to explore what it would be like to move to a 55+ community. We moved into the biggest and perhaps best established one, Laguna Woods in Orange County, California.

They had a huge art clubhouse, and because the community is so large, there are incredibly talented people in every field. Members taught classes in everything you could think of and other members usually attended these classes at little or no charge.

My husband was immediately recruited to teach computer classes and I was asked to teach beginner's drawing. Even after all the years of art lessons, I didn't consider drawing my strong point. Sooooo...I went into my growing art library and designed a curriculum that I believed could get anyone drawing with some confidence in a semester.

My non-traditional exercises were designed for fun and success. Some of the other teachers hung around in the room to see what I was doing. I felt judged initially. Then, something interesting began to happen. Experienced artists were joining the class "to brush up on their drawing" and others were asking for copies of my handouts. Students who initially came in to try one class started returning every week. Best of all, the painting teachers said they wanted to require all their students to take my class before they came to a painting class.

My reviews from the students were good and I was asked to teach the class again the next semester. One challenge I faced was having repeaters. I had to have alternative assignments for those who wanted to go further but had taken the class before.

The people were great, I made some good friends and it was fun to be able to design something that worked.

Since I could give a class that was free to residents, I could also take them. Enter Aurora Leos. Aurora and her husband had moved into the community at about the same time as we did. She had an art press that was too large for the place that she lived. She arranged with the management that she could leave her press in the art clubhouse, but no one could use it unless she was present. Aurora began to teach printmaking once a week. This was something I knew nothing about.

She was teaching a technique called drypoint etching, working with non-toxic inks made from a soy base and acrylic plates rather than copper which needed acid to complete the carving of plates. This was the most difficult art form I had ever attempted, but Aurora was a master printmaker. Her work was breathtaking, and she loved sharing with others. She limited the class size to about five, so everyone worked directly with her and everyone got press time.

Once I started, I was hooked. I never arrived at class without a new plate ready to ink and test on the press to see what I had accomplished. Printmaking is messy, takes up a lot of space, and requires learning many new techniques. For example, inking the plate is a science in itself. Some of the greats inked and pulled their own prints, while others took the plates to someone who had a good press and was a master at inking and creating the exact amount of pressure to make the best piece possible from the plate.

During the year, there were several competitions in the art clubhouse. Everyone participated and winning a ribbon wasn't easy because of the large number of accomplished and talented people in the community.

After studying with Aurora for some time, she encouraged me to enter one of my prints in one of these large shows. The competition was judged by a professor at the local fine arts academy in Laguna Beach, nearby. This commentary hung next to my work during the show with the judge's notes, with my first place ribbon.

Printmaking 1st Prize: "I found this drypoint etching intriguing; the repetition of the image of the woman (or is it women?) pulled me in. I read the title: 'She was smart before she married'. Wow! This is an artwork that forces the viewer to ask questions, to have a dialogue with the work. It makes you stand there and think about it."

Aurora and I both moved out of the community at about the same time. She moved out of state, and Victor and I moved to a house closer to family. I won't forget the many productive hours in the Laguna Woods Art Clubhouse, both teaching, and learning.

Change Your Thinking
Change Your Life

As a teacher/mentor is it more important to:

• Understand your role?

_____
_____
_____
_____
_____
_____
_____
_____
_____
_____
_____
_____
_____
_____

- Provide resources?

_____

_____

_____

_____

_____

_____

_____

_____

_____

_____

_____

_____

_____

_____

- Be collaborative?

_____

_____

_____

_____

_____

_____

_____

_____

_____

_____

_____

_____

_____

_____

_____

_____

- Follow through with your commitments?

_____

_____

_____

_____

_____

_____

_____

_____

_____

_____

_____

_____

_____

_____

_____

_____

_____

"I don't want to discount talent and ability, but I still maintain that a lot of it is just sheer desire."

— Don Henley

CHAPTER 11

A New Country, A Noted Mentor

Rainy Day Bar Beach

"No artist is ahead of his time. He is his time.
It is just that the others are behind the times."
— Martha Graham

*D*uring a difficult divorce, our daughter was trying to put her life back together. She got a job at Yosemite National Park in the research library and moved to a tiny rental cottage nearby with her youngest child who had one year to complete high school.

Her Yosemite job was part-time, so she trained to become a search and rescue volunteer. One day, when she was assigned to stand in front of a dangerous spot and keep tourists away from it, a man and his grown daughter came hiking by. He held a camera and wanted to get the perfect photo of one of the beautiful waterfalls in the park.

She explained that the area he wanted to enter was unsafe, but that she would take a picture of the two of them with his camera and help them to get safely back to their car. He suggested she get in the photo as well and she agreed if he would send her the picture. He then had her e-mail address and that began a year-long correspondence when he returned home to Australia.

Why am I telling you all this? The fact is, you never know when and where you are going to meet someone who will be important in your life. Volunteering to do something you love to do, such as search and rescue, or sitting on a non-profit board can be excellent places to meet that person.

What does this have to do with finding a mentor? Only that you never know where you will meet someone who can change your life.

When the Australian tourist heard that my daughter had a lifelong dream to dive the great barrier reef, he told her he was also a diver. She said that after her divorce was final, she wanted to do that dive. He offered to plan it for her.

This is a short version of explaining why I was in Australia, with a sick husband who could not travel, visiting my daughter and her new domestic partner...which leads to a story of how I found a wonderful art mentor in Newcastle, New South Wales, Australia.

In the case of the Australian tourist, my daughter now lives in Australia with a wonderful, kind, smart man who has had a big part in helping her to reclaim her life and live it with dignity again.

Victor and I planned a cruise to see our daughter and her partner at their home in Newcastle for a couple of weeks. It is said that "we plan, God Laughs." We moved into an Airbnb near their home and were enjoying our brief visit when my husband, Victor, had a massive heart attack and landed in the hospital in intensive care. The doctors told us that at the most, he had three weeks to live, but that is not what happened. Our short visit turned into 15 long months. As was my practice, I continued to paint every day, and my daughter encouraged me to find classes that I would enjoy, that would give me some time to myself.

There is a wonderful facility in Newcastle called the Hudson Street Hum. After trying a couple of classes there, I settled on one that I thought would be perfect for me. Unfortunately, when I called, the class was closed to new people. I contacted the teacher to explain my situation, but he said no. Then, my persuasive daughter called and told him about my work and he still said no. I don't know how long it took me to convince him to let me come to one class, but at last, he finally said yes.

That was how I met Peter Lankas, a superb artist and mentor who also became a friend. He helped me get through the most difficult year of my life.

Every week, Peter challenged me to try new techniques I had never done and often had never heard of before. I mean, who has heard of painting with powdered graphite and is it really a thing? Powdered graphite was a challenge but was fun to experiment with. Then, he taught a classical technique for painting portraits. I had never heard of it, and it enhanced my skills in mixing colors significantly.

Peter also got me involved in an evening life drawing class. This was tough and I wasn't good at it. Week after week, I returned and slowly improved.

He would stop by my workspace, look carefully, and almost whisper a tip that would explain how I could improve what I was doing.

Each morning at about 6 AM, I would go outside of the house the four of us were sharing and take photos of the sun rising over the ocean. I began a series of new paintings based on the photographs. Peter encouraged me to build the series and turn it into something that was different and new for me. When I was working, I felt challenged and happier. That sad time, during which my husband was dying, had bright spots in the week when my focus changed to improving my work. Whatever I painted, my husband enjoyed looking at and talking about it with me.

Then, there was that difficult life drawing class. It was as if I was back twenty years before, taking my first art lesson. I was terrible at it, but Peter kept saying to me that I should draw the way I paint.

There was an annual show of work done in the class. Peter told me that I didn't have to enter if I didn't want to. My response was, "You don't know me very well if you think I won't be ready for the show."

I stopped trying to draw like the people who had been in the group for years and got in touch with my own style, changing my focus to make the drawings look like I had done them. Each of us was allowed four entries in the show. The evening was wonderful, including the fact that my husband Victor came for a while. To top it off, I sold two of my pieces.

What changed? The support of a wonderful caring mentor who reminded me that I was an artist with a distinctive style, and I needed to do it my way to make it work.

The classes also allowed me to meet some wonderful Australian artists who became good friends, in addition to Peter and his wife Susan. As I watched Peter work with other artists in the same way, I was so impressed with him. He wasn't trying to make clones of himself. He was helping each of us to be better versions of ourselves, probably the definition of a good mentor.

We later laughed about my early attempts to get into his class. I often thanked him for taking me on and enriching the time I spent so far from home. He would respond that it made him feel good to have a student who worked so hard and got so much out of each session. What started with a difficult beginning turned into a mutual admiration society .

The Essence

The American Psychological Association lists characteristics of effective mentoring to include:

"The ability and willingness to:
- Value the mentee as a person
- Develop mutual trust and respect
- Maintain confidentiality
- Listen to what is being said and how
- Help the mentee solve his or her own problem
- Focus on the mentee's development and
- Resist the urge to produce a clone."

Peter personified this for me.

Change Your Thinking
Change Your Life

- Keep trying when you find someone who has something to teach you. How many times would you go back and fight if you thought you had found the perfect teacher?

_____

_____

_____

_____

_____

_____

_____

_____

_____

_____

_____

_____

- If you find that thing that becomes a real passion, how much time could you spend perfecting it so that it becomes a part of you?

_____

_____

_____

_____

_____

_____

_____

_____

_____

_____

_____

_____

_____

For me, painting became an everyday practice from the time I first started my lessons with Jayne and it continues through this year.

"I still have an insane drive to create and express myself, and it'll never stop because I don't know how to stop it."
— Graham Nash

CHAPTER 12

A Green Light Mentor

Stockton Sunrise

"The mentor-mentee relationship is a tango between a more senior person and a junior one. Just as in a dance, coordination and orchestration is necessary for grace and success."
— Vincent Chopra and Sanjay Saint

The following is a summary of Peter's thoughts on teaching. You will be able to evaluate his point of view in what he says. In addition, I have included a letter to a gallerist that finishes the Australia story.

Summary of Peter's introduction and philosophy of teaching artists

I run a small class with a maximum of 8 students, giving all plenty of one on one time with the tutor. Some artists have been attending for years.

Drawing is the most basic, primal visual representational language available to us. It is an underpinning element to all artistic practices and any creative person who has strengths in drawing will always have an edge above the rest. Anyone can draw or make art. It is a process like any other that can be learned with practice by all, developing a language to document and develop ideas.

The term will look at compositional elements as well as conceptual concerns of constructing imagery. Color theory will be covered as well as varied media use. Objective and subjective approaches to drawing will be covered as well as a varied selection of subject matter and genres

Ongoing and beyond, more complex conceptual and design elements will be covered to give a student the foundation to develop a deeper personal vision and technical approach to picture-making. Some students have been coming for a few terms or more and we experiment with deeper media and mixed approaches as well as developing a personal vision, selecting particular mediums and developing concepts.

On a regular basis, I do give demonstrations and give lessons in particular elements. Those who are interested can then work on these elements. It is a committed, focused, but a relaxed and easygoing atmosphere of creatives.

Some of my students have over time attended my solvent-free oil painting workshops in the tradition of the old masters. This year, I am hoping to focus more on the solvent-free oil methods for those who are interested.

As mentioned, the class has limited numbers so, "first in best dressed" as the old saying goes. If you have been trying to get into a class for a while, let me know and I will try to give you preference. I get hundreds of inquiries and sometimes lose track. In the long run, I can help you achieve your art goals in whatever medium or concept.

— Peter M. Lanka

Letter to a Gallerist

Dear D,

Thanks for your note. I don't know if you have heard the story of our adventures during the last year and a half. Victor and I left for a cruise with our daughter and her new Australian partner last January. Though my husband wasn't well, his doctors all said go and have fun. So, we flew to meet them in Auckland. We planned a two-week cruise, a few days to visit their home in Newcastle, NSW, Australia, and then home.

But, that didn't happen. Victor had a huge heart attack in Australia and many of the doctors there advised against flying home as they said it could make him even worse. At one point, they told us he had three weeks at the most to live. As it turned out, he lived for over a year longer. My daughter and her partner personally cared for his health and the two of us had many hours for reflection and discussion of our lives and our feelings.

We moved into a house that would hold the four of us, not the best situation for me, but we made the best of it. Then, in December, a neighbor asked if I would go with her to see her brother-in-law who was a chiropractor since I was not walking straight.

She saved my life, as he immediately sent me for an x-ray, and five days later on the 26th of December, I had major surgery to repair and replace seven vertebrae, basically rebuilding my neck. It turned into four surgeries when I contracted a hospital-based infection that was resistant to antibiotics. I ended up with a month-long hospitalization with the first three days in intensive care.

When Victor died in March, I booked one of the last two flights from Sydney to Los Angeles as all flights between the two countries were canceled due to the pandemic. I had two days to pack, get to the airport several hours away, and get home on a 17-hour flight.

I am currently having physical therapy twice a week, a visiting nurse comes once a week and I am seeing a new doctor who is monitoring my progress. My driver's license expired while I was gone, so I am trying to get an extension from the DMV, but no response to my request yet.

I am isolating with my son and his family. I am sleeping at home, then they pick me up to join them for dinner in the evening and bring me home at about 10:00 p.m.

You see, getting to you right now is probably not something I can accomplish with ease. I am hoping to be able to reconnect later in the year as we see what is happening in the world.

I do miss you all.

— Susan Soffer Cohn

Change Your Thinking
Change Your Life

Green Light Mentors

Have you found these qualities in your search for a mentor? If so, you are probably on the right track.

Which qualities are most important to you?

- They have real-life experience in your area of interest.
- They enjoy being part of other people's success
- They speak and act respectfully to others
- They are invested in the growth of themselves and others
- You and others like the person.
- They have and have had mentors themselves

_____

_____

_____

"It's a wrong idea that a master is a finished person. Masters are very faulty; they haven't learned everything, and they know it."
— **Robert Henri**

CHAPTER 13
History of Art Mentors
How the Greats Learned

Scott and Sabrina

"Every artist dips his brush in his own soul and paints his own nature into his pictures."

— Henry Ward

"Artistic growth is, more than anything else, a refining of the sense of truthfulness. The stupid believe that to be truthful is easy: only the great artist knows how difficult it is."

— Willa Cather

"The defining function of the artist is to cherish consciousness."

— Max Eastman

While studying art history, I have become aware of how many great artists learned their craft. Artists are often teachers and influencers of the ones that come after them. Here are some examples of some of the greats who learned and taught.

Andy Warhol influenced the way we viewed art, fame, and commercial culture in the twentieth century. Three main influences in his life turned him from a sickly child to an influential figure.

The first was his mother, Julia Warhol. The family moved from Czechoslovakia with three sons in 1921. Julia was an artist. Among the crafts that she sold were Campbell's Soup cans made into flowers.

Since Andy was ill, she provided him with art materials and encouraged him to draw. He often sat at the kitchen table drawing and eating Campbell's soup. Warhol moved to New York from Pittsburgh in 1952. His mother joined him two years later in an apartment filled with cats. The two each published a book that year with drawings of cats. Julia's book was signed "Andy Warhol's Mother." Julia's playful line drawing style influenced her son.

Warhol collected works and was influenced by Marcel Duchamp before the two met. Duchamp did a series of pieces which depicted ordinary objects long before Warhol did.

Warhol's third influence was Nathan Gluck. Gluck studied at Cooper Union and Art Students League. He and some fellow artists invited Warhol to show with them in the studio loft of another artist. He encouraged Warhol, though he was more conservative and had a successful career as an art director and graphic designer.

Of course, Warhol went on to create his own genre.

Georgia O'Keefe, the highest-selling woman artist at auction, taught drawing and penmanship in public schools in Amarillo, Texas from 1912 to 1914. She was famous for painting the beauty of the southwest with a feeling of sensuality.

Marc Chagall was also a teacher. In 1921, the Russian-French artist worked as an art teacher in a Jewish boys' war shelter in Malakovka, Russia. The shelter housed orphan refugees from Ukrainian pogroms.

Cezanne studied in Paris with impressionists Edouard Manet, Claude Monet, and most notably, Camille Pissaro, his most significant influence.

Pissaro also studied with great forerunners: Gustave Courbet and Jean-Baptiste Camille Corot. He later studied with George Seurat and Paul Signac at the age of 54.

George Seurat 1st studied with Justin Lequiene, a sculptor. Seurat attended the Ecole des Beaux-Arts in 1878 and 1879.

Michelangelo was apprenticed at age 13 to one of Florence's preeminent Renaissance artists, Domenico Ghirlandais, who was famous for his work in cathedrals and chapels in Italy. In 1489, he was chosen to attend a special school and studied with Bertoldo di Giovanni. This was a fertile time for Michelangelo, permitting him access to the social life of Florence.

Bertoldo di Giovanni studied with Donatello, who would subsequently teach many of Italy's famous Renaissance sculptors.

Leonardo studied with Andrea del Verrocchio. Much of his early training was also spent in the service of Ludovico il Moro in Milan. He received training in painting, sculpture, and technical mechanical drawing. He died in 1519 after working in Rome, Bologna, and Venice.

This is a little indication of the "ladder." Every artist stands on the shoulders of those who came before and often had students or apprentices who were taught the skills and went on to become significant artists.

A Few More Stories Regarding My Journey

White Horse

I Cried on My 50thBirthday

It's a little embarrassing looking back on my 50th birthday. I had an appointment for a physical that day and walked into the doctor's office crying.

My children were grown, I had had a long and interesting career, had completed an MBA degree, but that day I believed that the learning, the growth, and the surprises were over. Fifty seemed old to me that day. Having always been an optimist, this does not appear to fit, but believe me, it happened.

My doctor started telling me stories about other patients, emphasizing my health and my life, and assuring me that my life was just beginning. Though I walked in crying, I walked out laughing. Since that day, I have been gratefully aware that every morning brings a new day with new possibilities and lessons.

Price High if you Don't Want to Sell?

After our last move to the Los Angeles South Bay area, I was introduced to a wonderful group of artists called The Artists' Studio of Palos Verdes. They had been running a gallery/gift shop at the Palos Verdes Art Center for 30 years. New artist applications are reviewed by a jury of members to assure a high level of quality of work in order to participate in the many opportunities for showing and selling artwork.

During my first year in the group, I sold more pieces of my art than all the rest of the years put together.

One of the annual events is an artist studio tour. My studio was on the tour during the first tour after I joined. I asked my son, an art collector, to come over and help me price and display the paintings for the event.

I had a large mixed media piece on the wall by the entry and I didn't want to take it down, but I didn't think I wanted to sell it. My son said to price it high and no one would want to buy it. He priced it at $11,000. About halfway through the first day, a man approached me, put his hands over his heart and said he had to have the piece. He asked me to write a contract between us that when he returned from an extended business trip, he would purchase it.

Is the moral of the story, if you want to sell it, put a high price on it? Or did the price attract attention? I don't know.

Making Non-toxic Oils

When I was working with Peter Lankas, I took his workshop on making non-toxic oil paints. I really enjoyed the way the paint moved and looked, so I decided to jump in with both feet and start the long process of purifying natural oils and making my own paints. Peter made it look easy, but it wasn't for me. Just preparing the oil took weeks and weeks. They had to be in a carefully prepared container and left outside in the sun for weeks, stirring regularly. After the three-week point, it was time to bring the jars inside and do the next step. I picked up two of the jars and asked Lawrence, my daughter's partner, to please hand me the third. Lawrence picked up the jar, saw a giant cockroach inside, and thought it was waste, so he dumped it out before handing it to me. Three weeks down the drain.

I had to laugh. He didn't have any idea that I had been nursing these jars along for weeks. As I examine the situation, I am certain I could have done a better job of explaining what I needed, or I could have taken the two inside and come back for the third. I did salvage about ½ inch of oil from that container and had plenty to proceed in the two other jars.

Making your own oil paints is definitely an adventure. In my first attempt, I did not create paints that were nearly as wonderful as Peter's samples that I used in the workshop. I could not bring them on the plane with me when I returned to the USA. Perhaps I will try again sometime.

CHAPTER 14

Own Your Dreams and Begin Your Adventure

The Touch 2

"Art washes away from the soul the dust of everyday life."

— Pablo Picasso

If you think this book is about me, you may be missing the point. It is true that what I have been sharing with you in the previous chapters is my journey, but my purpose in sharing it is to guide you toward finding your own passion and getting help to pursue it and succeed in living a fuller life.

Try new things. The world is full of opportunities and the only barriers exist in our heads. Believe in yourself. Limiting your options is not something someone else does to you. The only person who can hold you back is you.

As I have grown older, my body shouts in pain and my heart grows heavier with loss. My solace and peace are found with my personal challenge of creating what I see and feel on a canvas. I can stand for hours concentrating on painting, I find inner peace and smile with my accomplishment, even if it is small.

Thomas Merton expressed the above so well, "Art enables us to find ourselves and lose ourselves at the same time."

How do you begin to set goals? A goal should be realistic, challenging, specific, measurable, and timely.

Determine why you want to accomplish your goal and visualize what it will look like when you achieve it. Break large goals into smaller action steps. Keep your focus on the end result. Then, check your progress regularly on a dated chart so you can keep track of your progress.

My Challenge to You

Thanks for accompanying me on this journey. It is my hope that my adventure will inspire yours. I have prepared some tools for you to use for that purpose.

First, go back through the book and answer the questions at the end of the chapters. Second, order my free E-book download of my goal-setting process. Set aside a couple of hours to do the exercises. Writing your goals properly is an incredible tool for getting you to the next step in your life. You are important enough to do this. Making this exercise a priority is critical to making yourself and your future your priority. I know you can do it, which is why I have created these tools for you to use in your growth process.

Change Your Thinking Change Your Life

Here is what I suggest as you search for what it is you want in life.

- Set goals and then find green light mentors to help you get where you want to go.

- Can you write down two goals that will lead you in a direction that you want to go?

1. _____

   _____

   _____

   _____

2. _____

   _____

   _____

   _____

3. _____

   _____

   _____

- Have you written in a measurable goal with a date for achieving it?

_____

_____

_____

_____

_____

_____

_____

_____

_____

_____

_____

_____

_____

_____

_____

_____

_____

- Write down some small steps that will help you to accomplish your goal.

_____

_____

_____

_____

_____

_____

_____

_____

_____

_____

_____

_____

_____

_____

_____

Own Your Dreams and Begin Your Adventure

- What obstacles might keep you from reaching these goals?

_____

_____

_____

_____

_____

_____

_____

_____

_____

_____

_____

_____

_____

_____

_____

- Set deadlines for accomplishment of the goals and evaluating the results.

_____

_____

_____

_____

_____

_____

_____

_____

_____

_____

_____

_____

_____

_____

_____

_____

"Every artist dips his brush in his own soul and paints his own nature into his pictures."
— Henry Ward Beecher

Koala Sketch

In Memorium

Runner

On March 19th, 2020 at approximately 6 AM, my husband of 57 years took his last breath. He was so very ill that I didn't want him to continue to suffer but giving up his encouragement and daily loving support has not been easy for me.

He was, among other things, the computer guru for family and friends. He started in computers in his 20's and did some award-winning development work over the years. I am left with a room full of technology that I don't know how to master. If the computer doesn't balk, I can do the basic things I need to do. I fight with the equipment on a daily basis, especially as I work to complete this book.

Roles

In the '50s, most of us grew up hearing that the only possible careers for women included being a secretary, a teacher, or a nurse. In my family, these were not acceptable occupations, but staying home was. My mom mainly drove carpools, led our Brownie troop, played cards, and hung out with friends.

I was not expected to do anything differently. I guess it was considered my job to find a husband who could support me in the "manner in which I had become accustomed."

Of course, even in our upscale community, few young men had the resources in their 20's to do that.

That's what I heard, but what did I see?

I saw my hard-working grandmother, not only running her business but running the whole family...a beloved powerhouse. She took me to work with her as I was growing up. It was a place I always felt happy and comfortable.

Largely because of my grandmother, I attended an all-girls camp for eight weeks each for seven summers. Burr Oaks Camp emphasized leadership training and achievement programs. We started as little girls and advanced to leaders when we were almost out of high school. There were no boys there. We didn't have to let anyone be the winners but us, so we were taught to go for the top.

When I got to high school, some wonderful teachers encouraged us. Fortunately, the Clayton school I attended was one of the best in the state.

I had a French teacher who inspired us by telling us that someday, we would have breakfast in St. Louis, lunch in New York and dinner in Paris, and she fully expected us to do so. At the top of the teacher list was my first feminist,

Mr. Blandford Jennings. Not a young man, Mr. Jennings was one of the most forward-thinking people I had ever met. I was in his senior honors English class. Twenty of us sat around heavy wood tables and were challenged daily to excel.

We had no textbooks and no grammar lessons. All of us had passed our grammar tests before we got to high school. We read literature and were pushed to achieve with constant writing assignments. One day while reading a passage from some of the best papers in the class, he addressed the girls by telling us not to waste our brains.

After high school, I was off to a woman's college, with high standards. Our professors told us we were among the brightest. Today's students might interpret the message as "girls rule."

I was only 19 when Victor wanted to get married . I wasn't sure I was ready and went to the counselling office at Washington University, where I had transferred to be closer to home. We got married the following summer at the age of twenty.

Married women were supposed to cook and clean and worst of all, iron. One day, my cousin Rachel came over and we spent an entire afternoon trying to iron a set of monogrammed cotton sheets. They looked just as bad when we finished as when we started. After that experience, sheets were sent to the laundry…that is until permanent press sheets arrived on the horizon a short time later.

That was only one of the domestic chores I was not prepared for and we argued about in that first year of marriage. Somehow, we survived it, though I never became a domestic goddess. We were both full-time students. We were both working to pay our bills. The good news was that my grades were the best they ever were, despite our period of adjustment.

In my senior year, my journalism professor handed out a paper to the women-only called, "How to be a Good Editorial Assistant." I was horrified. It said we would not be able to get editorial jobs, so we needed to know how to be promoted. He made up for it, however, when he recommended me for my first job as an editor.

When it came to being a mother, there was nothing I thought was more important. My children were my treasure and my primary concern.

In the end, the story for us about sex roles turned out to be the following. I was probably one of the most fortunate women to grow up during the fifties. I had strong female role models and teachers who encouraged me to be everything I could. I married a man who was capable of growing and changing with me. Together, we were part of a changing world in the sixties. I'm proud that we led the way, finding new models for what a marriage should look like. We had a true partnership with each of us doing the things we loved and did well, instead of the things others expected of us.

Appendix

Press-Telegram FRIDAY · JANUARY 26, 2007

By Shirle Gottlieb
Special to the Press-Telegram

GATOV GICLEE

"Inspired by New Circles," an exhibit of work by Susan Soffer Cohn, is on view at the Gatov Gallery through Feb. 5.

Though paintings and mixed-media collages are part of her body of work, Cohen specializes in Giclee prints.

Giclee prints are high fidelity reproductions (with high resolution) that are individually produced on special presses. Cohen has a nice fresh way of handling her prints, as she demonstrates in several colorful abstract expressionistic works that include "Exodus," "The Sanctity of Marriage" and "Orchids."

The blue brushwork in her acrylic painting "Victoria Falls I" is reminiscent of the swirling sky in Van Gogh's "Starry Night" while the loveliest mixed-media collage on display is "Shoreline," a poetic splash of purple, blue and green wildflowers that line the river bank. There's also a case of handmade jewelry constructed from beads, semi-precious stones, silver, glass, and mah jong tiles.

Susan Soffer Cohen, Gatov Gallery, Alpert Jewish Community Center, 3601 E. Willow St., Long Beach; (562) 426-7601. 9 a.m.-10 p.m. Monday-Thursday, 9 a.m.-6 p.m. Friday, 10 a.m.-6 p.m. Saturday and Sunday; through Feb. 5.

Susan Soffer Cohn's mixed-media geometric abstract "New Circles" is part of her exhibit at the Gatov Gallery in the Long Beach Jewish Community Center.

MUSEUMS & GALLERIES

Continuing

Alpert Jewish Community Center, Gatov Gallery, 3801 E. Willow St., Long Beach, (562) 426-7601. 9 a.m.-10 p.m. Monday-Thursday, 9 a.m.-6 p.m. Friday and 10 a.m.-6 p.m. Saturday and Sunday. "Inspired by New Circles" features paintings and mixed media works by Susan Soffer Cohn; through Feb. 5.

MAY 2009

Orange County Fine Arts — Artist's Eye

A Non-Profit Organization • 3851 S. Bear St., Suite B-15; Santa Ana, CA 92704 • 714-540-6430 • orangecountyfinearts.com

SUSAN SOFFER COHN TO DEMONSTRATE 'COMAGE' AT MAY 28 MEETING

Using her unique style combining collage and assemblage with the aesthetic underpinnings of both Eastern and Western traditional art, our May demonstrator **Susan Soffer Cohn** creates layered, textural works that can range from representational to mystical to abstract.

"Comage" is her term, and her influences run from Picasso and Kandinsky to Rauschenberg and Judy Chicago. Her method is essentially intuitive. "I often start," says Susan, "without knowing where I am going and the canvas tells me what I need. One layer speaks to the next, begging for a touch to complete it, ,and it lets me know. When this happens, I willingly give myself over to the excitement of the instant and let the work come through me instead of from me."

She received a BA in Journalism from the University of Washington and her MBA from Pepperdine University, Malibu. Later she

attended Desert Fine Arts Academy, studying with **Jayne Behman, David Einstein** and **Harvey Silverman**. She also attended workshops given by **Stephen Quiller, BJ Wilson** and **Milford Zornes**.

A resident of Huntington Beach, Susan has exhibited widely both in Orange County and the desert communities, winning awards at Huntington Harbor Art Association, Cypress Art League, Huntington Beach Art League, National Date Festival, India, Palm Springs Museum Artist Council Show, Palm Springs City Show, as well as Lake Arrowhead Rotary Show and the Central Coast National Show at Morro Bay.

Susan has had solo shows at the 7007 Gallery in Whittier, the Huntington Beach Main Library Gallery, The Pauline & Zena Gatov Gallery in Long Beach, and Vista Event at Long Beach Jewish Federation in 2006.

Susan has been asked to do a show at the Museo Civico di Abano Terme (Padua, Italy) beginning September 10, 2009, and she has also been invited to participate in the Huntington Bearch Art Center Plein Air Festival again this year.

We hope you can join us May 28 for this very unique demonstration.

Susan Soffer Cohn will demonstrate her unique technique at our May meeting

Orange County Fine Arts Inc. is a non-profit corporation that seeks to stimulate community interest in the Fine Arts by providing special programs, exhibits and demonstrations by well-known artists; to furnish a place for viewing works of art; and to provide scholarships to deserving art students. Membership is open to anyone; there are no restrictions.

"Comage"...the art of layering

View the innovative artwork
of Susan Soffer Cohn at the {Solo} exhibit

Artexpo Las Vegas
Booth # S320

Friday, September 28, 12 to 6 P.M.
Saturday, September 29, 11 A.M.to 6 P.M.
Sunday, September 30, 11 A.M. to 5 P.M.

Mandalay Bay Resort & Casino
3950 Las Vegas Blvd. South
Las Vegas, NV 89119

Contact:
devon@blainegroupinc.com
cohnart@yahoo.com
vicvac86@yahoo.com

Please let us know if you want a VIP pass

"THEME AND VARIATION IN GREEN"

"COMAGE" BY SUSAN SOFFER COHN

Striations

by Susan Soffer Cohn

Susan Soffer Cohn's

"Blue Lady"

Will be on exhibit at the
Fyr Gallery
Florence, Italy
September 4 to 30, 2009

and

Susan Soffer Cohn's
Comage© abstracts, including
Striations,
will be one of her 15 works in an
international show at the
Museo Civico di Abano Terme
Abano Terme, Italy
Opens September 10, 2009
Continues for one month

Contact:
devon@blainegroupinc.com
cohnart@yahoo.com
vicvac86@yahoo.com

171

❧ 10 ❧

REMARKABLE
DESERT WOMEN

SUSAN COHN:

The Gift Inside

By Elizabeth Carroll

*S*usan Cohn has a passion for painting. Who knew?

Certainly not the successful, self-effacing Susan who parlayed a journalism degree and an MBA into a career as writer/editor/publicist focusing on clients in the health care and banking fields.

Susan Cohn
Photo by Kate Porter

Now, less than two years after discovering that "painting is my core," this prolific artist has had several exhibitions; her work has appeared in juried shows (even winning an honorable mention); and countless tourists and locals have seen, even had their pictures taken on, the bench she created for the now-on-hold Palms Springs Art ~ Bench Project.

Moving to Palm Springs from Beverly Hills four years ago, when her husband Victor retired, one goal was to write a children's story for her six "exceptional" grandchildren. She joined the Palm Springs Writers Guild. It was suggested that the resultant children's story needed illustrations.

Enter serendipity. A fundraiser with a silent auction. Victor was top bidder on four art lessons for her with Jayne Behman.

To say that Susan became enthralled is an understatement. By the end of the sessions she was hooked on art. Jayne suggested painting classes.

"She's done so much for me," enthuses Susan. "She showed me the wonderful gift inside me that I didn't know existed."

Jayne was embarking on the Bench Project as a fundraiser for the Desert Fine Arts Foundation. Susan was a willing advocate. The Public Arts Commission gave approval for a test of the concept.

A design Susan submitted was chosen.

Now came the real challenge. How to paint on concrete ("it was like doing nine paintings") and how to meet a July deadline. Oh yes, there was the little matter of painting outdoors in 107 degrees. Victor rented a crane, had the 1800-pound bench moved to their garage and strung up lights so she could paint at night.

❧ 11 ❧

REMARKABLE
DESERT WOMEN

The bench was installed in the 700 block of North Palm Canyon Drive. She entitled the work, "Healing Pond," but is delighted when viewers put their own interpretation on the colorful creation. "I don't like to label my style," she says, "abstract, perhaps loose."

Her first exhibition, for a First Friday Gallery Walk, led to several more. And to sales.

With other cancer survivors (her bout was with thyroid cancer), Susan exhibited at the Relay for Life in November. She found this event "a bit overwhelming." Her daughter, Melissa, was completing breast cancer radiation treatments the same day.

An ambitious ongoing project is her "Joseph" series of paintings (he of the many-colored coat) with a biblical, spiritual theme ~ "Exodus," "Burning Bush," "Sodom and Gomorrah." "I'm working toward an exhibition in an appropriate setting." Meanwhile, her work can be seen on Feb. 22 at the "Kaleidoscope 2003" juried exhibition at The River in Rancho Mirage. Three of Susan's paintings, "Many Moons," "Star Dance Over Palm Springs," and "Joseph 11," are on display until Feb 27 at the Palm Springs City Hall as part of the Fifth Annual Juried "Palm Springs Paints and Shoots."

Art has added a new discipline to Susan's life. "It's forced me into having a to-do list." That list includes the Palm Springs Writers Guild, Hadassah, and Steps for Kids, a foundation she and Victor are creating with the hope of "broadening children's minds so they have a path to the future, giving them self-esteem."

And then there's genealogy, another ardent interest. She gives workshops, teaches the simple rules of family trees. "It's a fun time with lots of audience participation." And she writes a family history column in the *Jewish Community News*. She got into this area after tracing her family back eight generations. "I come from a family of incredible women who were educated long before this was the norm, who were successful in their own businesses when most women stayed home, women who impacted many lives."

This Desert Woman has not strayed far from family tradition.

Elizabeth Carroll is a writer and part-time desert resident. Although a permanent resident of Merritt, British Columbia, during her many trips to the Coachella Valley she has written prolifically, including an entire series on historical desert women which appeared in several past issues of "The Desert Woman."

Art and Philanthropy:

A Winning Combination

Josh Kaplan

Susan Cohn's art is vibrant and tactile. She uses mixed media to convey images that evoke deep emotion and spirituality. Looking at her work, one may assume that she honed her style over a lifetime of drawing and painting. But Susan, a successful writer and editor with a journalism degree and an MBA, discovered her artistic gift when she was already a grandmother. At the time, she and her husband, Victor, were living in Palm Springs. They attended a fundraiser with a silent auction where Victor was the winning bidder on a set of four art lessons. By the end of those lessons, Susan says, she discovered "the wonderful gift inside me that I didn't know existed."

Susan's art will be on display at a one woman show enti-tled Images of our Traditions; Images of the West at The Corner Gallery in Huntington Beach. The Corner Gallery is a lovely space in the Huntington Beach Central Library. Susan and Victor are hosting a wine and cheese reception on Saturday, June 3, from 5 – 8 pm. The entire community is invited to celebrate the opening of the show and to enjoy the works of art displayed. Susan and Victor aren't just art enthusiasts; they're committed to Jewish philanthropy as well. In fact, a portion of the proceeds from the sales at the event will be donated to the Jewish Federation of Greater Long Beach and West Orange County. What a wonderful example of living generously!

The Corner Gallery at the Huntington Beach Library is located on Talbert, between Gothard and Goldenwest. For more information on this event, please contact Barbara Lieberman, Federation Campaign Director, at 562-426-7601 or blieberman@jewishlongbeach.org. For more information about Susan Cohn's art, please visit www.susancohnartist.com. Her work is featured on pages 8 and 9.

The Anti-Defamation gue recently held it nual National Lead Conference in Washi D.C. This annual confe brings together ADL l ship from around the to meet with internatior litical leaders, diploma thinkers. During the g ing, ADL presented its iel R. Ginsberg Lead Award. This coveted av presented annually to Jewish leaders who shown exemplary lead in their community th involvement with the A

For the first time in its ty-five year history, a from the Orange C Long Beach region re the award. Josh Kap Long Beach resident, w ognized for his extraor commitment to ADL. J chaired, with his wife St the Steinberg Leadersh stitute. In this role, he pr over a significant growth program and was influer bringing new leadershi the Jewish community. has supported the Le diversity education pro and worked to bring tion to ADL's work com hate/bias related behavi

In concert with Ste Josh is now" headin; leadership group's a

SAVE THE DATE
NOVEMBER 12-15, 2006

The annual UJC General Assembley will be held in Los Angeles this year!

Jewish Federation/Community Foundation

Reviews of the Artist, Susan Cohn

Art and Philanthropy: A Review

A Winning Combination

Susan Cohn's art is vibrant and tactile. She uses mixed media to convey images that evoke deep emotion and spirituality. Looking at her work, one may assume that she honed her style over a lifetime of drawing and painting. But, Susan, a successful writer, and editor with a journalism degree and an MBA discovered her artistic gift when she was already a grandmother. At the time, she and her husband Victor were living in Palm Springs. They attended a fundraiser with a silent auction where Victor was the winning bidder on a series of four art lessons. By the end of these lessons, Susan says she discovered "the wonderful gift inside me, that I didn't know existed."

Susan's art will be on display at a one-woman show entitled "Images of our Traditions: Images of the West" at the Corner Gallery in Huntington Beach. The Corner Gallery is a lovely space in the Huntington Beach Central Library. Susan and Victor are hosting a wine and cheese reception on Saturday, June 3, from 5 – 8 pm. The entire community is invited to celebrate the opening of the show and to enjoy the works of art displayed. Susan and Victor aren't just art enthusiasts; they're committed to Jewish philanthropy as well. In fact, a portion of the proceeds from sales at the event will be donated to the Jewish Federation of Greater Long Beach and West Orange County. What a wonderful example of living generously.

The Corner Gallery at the Huntington Beach Library is located on Talbert, between Gothard and Goldenwest. For more information on this event-------For more information about Susan Cohn's art visit www.Susancohnartist.com.

Susan Soffer Cohn to Demonstrate 'comage' on May 28th Meeting

Using her unique style combining collage and assemblage with the aesthetic underpinnings of both Eastern and Western traditional art, the May demonstrator, Susan Soffer Cohn, creates layered, textural works that can range from representational to mystical to abstract.

'Comage' is her term and her influences run from Pablo Picasso and Kandinsky to Rauschenberg and Judy Chicago. Her method is essentially intuitive. "I often start," says Susan, "without knowing where I am going and the canvas tells me what I need. One layer speaks to the next, begging for a touch to complete it, and it lets me know. When this happens, I willingly give myself over to the excitement of the instant and let the work come through me instead of from me."

She received her BA in English from Washington University in St. Louis and her MBA from Pepperdine University, Malibu. Later, she attended Desert Fine Arts Academy studying with Jayne Behman, David Einstein, and Harvey Silverman. She also attended workshops with Stephen Quiller, BJ Wilson, and Milford Zornes.

A resident of Huntington Beach, Susan has exhibited widely both in Orange County and the desert communities, winning awards at Huntington Harbor Art Association, Cypress Art League, Huntington Beach Art League, National Date Festival, Indio, Palm Springs Museum Artists' Council Show, Palm Springs City Show, as well as the Lake Arrowhead Rotary Show and the Central Coast National Show in Morro Bay.

Susan has had solo shows at the 7007 Gallery in Whittier, the Huntington Beach Central Library Corner Gallery, The Pauline and Zena Gatov Gallery in Long Beach, and the Vista event at Long Beach Jewish Federation.

Susan has been asked to do a show at the Museo Civico di Abano Terme (Padua, Italy) beginning September 10, 2009, and she has also been invited to participate in the Huntington Beach Art Center Invitational Plein Air Festival again this year. We hope you can join us for this very unique demonstration.

Remarkable Desert Women

SUSAN COHN: THE GIFT INSIDE

By Elizabeth Carroll

Susan Cohn has a passion for painting. Who knew?

Certainly not the successful, self-effacing Susan who parlayed a journalism degree and an MBA into a career as writer/editor/publicist focusing on clients in the healthcare and banking fields.

Now, less than two years after discovering that "painting is my core," this prolific artist has had several exhibitions; her work has appeared in juried shows, and countless tourists and locals have seen, even had their pictures taken on the bench she created for the now-on-hold Palm Springs Art.

Moving to Palm Springs from Beverly Hills four years ago when her husband Victor retired, her one goal was to write a children's story for her six "exceptional" grandchildren. She joined the Palm Springs Writers' Guild where it was suggested that the resultant children's story needed illustrations.

Enter serendipity. A fundraiser with a silent auction. Victor was the top bidder on four art lessons for her with Jayne Behman.

To say that Susan became enthralled is an understatement. By the end of the sessions, she was hooked on art. Jayne suggested painting classes.

"She's done so much for me," enthuses Susan. "She showed me the wonderful gift inside me that I didn't know existed."

Jayne was embarking on the Bench Project as a fundraiser for the Desert Fine Arts Foundation. Susan was a willing advocate. The Public Arts Commission approved a test of the concept.

A design submitted by Susan was chosen.

Now came the real challenge. How to paint concrete ("it was like doing nine paintings.") and how to meet a July deadline. Oh yes, there was a little matter of painting outdoors in 107 degrees. Victor rented a crane, had the 1800-pound bench moved to their garage, and strung up lights so she could paint at night.

The bench was installed in the 700 block of North Palm Canyon Drive. She entitled the work, "Healing Pond," but is delighted when viewers put their own interpretation on the colorful creation. "I don't like to label my style," she says, "abstract, perhaps loose."

Her first exhibition, for a First Friday Gallery Walk, led to several more. And to sales.

With other cancer survivors (her bout was with thyroid cancer), Susan exhibited at the Relay for Life in November. She found the event "a little overwhelming." Her daughter, Melissa, was completing breast cancer radiation treatments the same day.

An ambitious ongoing project is her "Joseph" series of paintings (he of the many-colored coat) with a biblical, spiritual theme—"Exodus", "Burning Bush", "Sodom and Gomorrah." "I'm working toward an exhibition in an appropriate setting." Meanwhile, her work can be seen on Feb. 22 at the "Kaleidoscope 2003" juried exhibition at The River in Rancho Mirage. Three of Susan's paintings, "Many Moons", "Star Dance Over Palm Springs" and "Joseph 11" are on display at the Palm Springs City Hall as part of the Fifth Annual Juried Palm Springs Paints and Shoots.

Art has added a new discipline to Susan's life. "It's forced me into having a to-do list." That list includes the Palm Springs Writer's Guild, Hadassah, and Steps for Kids, a foundation she and Victor are creating with the hope of "broadening children's minds so they have a path to the future, giving them self-esteem."

And then there's genealogy, another ardent interest. She gives workshops and teaches the simple rules of family trees. "It's a fun time with lots of audience participation." She also writes a family history column in the Jewish Community News. She got into this area after tracing her family back eight generations. "I come from a family of incredible women who were educated long before it was the norm, who were successful in their own businesses when most women stayed home, women who impacted many lives."

This Desert Woman has not strayed far from family traditions.

ON VIEW

By Shirle Gottlieb
Gatov Giclee

"Inspired by New Circles," an exhibit of work by Susan Cohn, is on view at the Gatov Gallery through Feb. 5th.

Though paintings and mixed media collages are part of her body of work, Cohn specializes in Giclee prints.

The blue brushwork in her acrylic painting 'VICTORIA FALLS I" is reminiscent of the swirling sky of Van Gogh's "Starry Night" while the loveliest mixed media collage on display is "Shoreline," a poetic splash of purple, blue and green wildflowers that line the riverbank.

Work with Susan

Horse Etching

Option #1 Setting Goals that Work

Susan Soffer Cohn is an author, artist, and teacher who lives in Redondo Beach, California. To reach her, send an e-mail to cohnart@yahoo.com and/or friend her on Facebook.

She will be happy to send you her free introduction to effective goal setting, Setting Goals That Work. Send her a request by e-mail.

Option #2 Vision Board Home Kit

Susan gives in-person vision board workshops to help the participants focus on the life they really want. You can purchase a Vision Board in a Box, an individual home workshop that includes supplies and instructions.

Contact Susan at cohnart@yahoo.com to get the price and order your at- home Vision Board Kit. A Vision Board is a great way to find your direction.

Susan will also arrange a group Vision Board workshop for your group. Contact her for further information.

She is also available for speaking on the topics covered in the book, as well as providing full-day workshops to groups on finding your passion and finding a mentor.

In addition, Susan is available for a private consultation. For further information, you can contact her at *1 714 702 9799*.

Giving a Workshop

Vision Board Workshop.... students model with results

Option #3 Engage Susan as your next Speaker

Susan Soffer Cohn is an internationally known and collected, award-winning, artist. Her work is in collections throughout the USA, Europe and Australia.

Author of "The Art of the Mentor," she reveals in her book her journey as an artist who found and finally became a mentor to others. All of this happened after she took her first art lesson after she turned 50.

Her work has appeared in Professional Artist Magazine in the USA and Australian Artist magazine in addition to other publications, both print and online. Now, Susan is sharing her amazing story and experiences to audiences across the country.

Based in sunny California, Susan's relaxed, and engaging style leaves her audiences inspired and ready to take on any challenge. A natural storyteller, Susan easily connects with her audience and her calm, considered presence is suited to those that are sick of the hype without substance speakers.

Susan specializes in the following topics which include:

- How to Leverage Your Visibility by Setting Goals
- How to Find and Be a Good Mentor
- Make a Vision Board to Find Your Focus
- You Can be an Artist Even if You Can't Draw a Straight Line
- The One Hour Abstract (an interactive seminar for any number of people)

To enquire about engaging Susan to speak at your next event or group get together, please email cohnart@yahoo.com for cost and availability.

About the Author

Atmosphere

Susan Soffer Cohn grew up in a huge family of parents, grandparents, aunts, uncles, and cousins, all of whom shared their interests and supported the other members of the family in whatever they pursued. Because of this, her early childhood involved a lot of mentoring from her many, many close relatives. An example of the size of her family is that 500 people were invited to her wedding, and almost all were close relatives.

One grandmother took her to see historic houses, the other took her to work, so she learned about business. An aunt introduced her to classical music and a great aunt took her to the opera and the theater.

Focusing on experimental art, her work has been exhibited throughout the United States and Europe and in Australia. Her work has also been featured in Professional Artist Magazine in the USA and Australian Artist Magazine.

Susan began painting at 50 and studied with carefully chosen mentors who were talented artists as well as master teachers. She currently lives in the Los Angeles South Bay area. She has painted daily for over 20 years.

As Susan discovered her fulfilling life as an artist, she now dreams of helping the people she meets to find out what their passion is and to meet mentors to help them to make their dreams come true.

You can talk to her about how she plans to do this by sending her an e-mail at Cohnart@yahoo.com Check out her website at Cohnart.com

The *Art of* The *Mentor*

The Superpower That Turns Good into Great

To enquire about engaging Susan to speak at your next event or group get together, please email **cohnart@yahoo.com** for cost and availability.

CONTACT SUSAN:
- ✉ cohnart@yahoo.com
- ⌨ www.cohnart.com
- ☎ 1 714 702 9799

SUSAN SOFFER COHN

is an internationally known and collected, award-winning, artist. Her work is in collections throughout the USA, Europe and Australia. Author of **"The Art of the Mentor,"** she reveals in her book her journey as an artist who found and finally became a mentor to others. All of this happened after she took her first art lesson after she turned 50. Her work has appeared in Professional Artist Magazine in the USA and Australian Artist magazine in addition to other publications, both print and online. Now, **Susan** is sharing her amazing story and experiences to audiences across the country. Based in sunny California, **Susan's** relaxed, and engaging style leaves her audiences inspired and ready to take on any challenge. A natural storyteller, **Susan** easily connects with her audience and her calm, considered presence is suited to those that are sick of the hype without substance speakers.

Susan specializes in the following topics which include:
- How to Leverage Your Visibility by Setting Goals
- How to Find and Be a Good Mentor
- Make a Vision Board to Find Your Focus
- You Can be an Artist Even if You Can't Draw a Straight Line
- The One Hour Abstract (an interactive seminar for any number of people)

Susan SOFFER *Cohn*

195

Acknowledgments

"All large tasks are completed in a series of starts."

— Neil Fiore

I would like to thank Natasa Denman and The Ultimate 48 Hour Author Team for their patience and assistance in helping me to make this book happen. Stuart, thanks for your personal input and to rockstar Vivi thanks for making it appear that I understand tech. In addition, Sabrina and Mary have been invaluable in doing edits upon edits when I couldn't look at a chapter one more time. My husband Victor always encouraged me. I could not have done this without him. Special thanks, to Scott, Kirby and Bonnie, who always believed in me and to Barbara Janes, Larry Baum and Blandford Jennings. As already indicated I am so grateful to Jayne, BJ, Peter, Aurora, David and Sidney.

Notes

Notes

Notes

Notes

Notes

CPSIA information can be obtained
at www.ICGtesting.com
Printed in the USA
FSHW020724201120

9 781922 497284